Different Croaks
for
Different Folks

of related interest

Can I tell you about Asperger Syndrome?
A guide for friends and family
Jude Welton
Foreword by Elizabeth Newson
Illustrated by Jane Telford
ISBN 1 84310 206 4

Different Like Me
My Book of Autism Heroes
Jennifer Elder
Illustrated by Marc Thomas and Jennifer Elder
ISBN 1 84310 815 1

Special Brothers and Sisters
Stories and Tips for Siblings of Children
with Special Needs, Disability or Serious Illness
Edited by Annette Hames and Monica McCaffrey
ISBN 1 84310 383 4

What Did You Say? What Do You Mean?
An Illustrated Guide to Understanding Metaphors
Jude Welton
Foreword by Elizabeth Newson
Illustrated by Jane Telford
ISBN 1 84310 207 2

Blue Bottle Mystery
An Asperger Adventure
Kathy Hoopmann
ISBN 1 85302 978 5

Of Mice and Aliens
An Asperger Adventure
Kathy Hoopmann
ISBN 1 84310 007 X

Buster and the Amazing Daisy
Nancy Ogaz
ISBN 1 84310 721 X

Different Croaks
for
Different Folks

All about Children with
Special Learning Needs

Midori Ochiai

With notes on developmental differences by Shinya Miyamoto

Illustrations by Hiroko Fujiwara

Translated by Esther Sanders

Jessica Kingsley Publishers
London and Philadelphia

Originally published in Japan by Tokyo Shoseki Co., Ltd., Tokyo
Translated from the Japanese by Esther Sanders

First published in English in 2006
by Jessica Kingsley Publishers
116 Pentonville Road
London N1 9JB, UK
and
400 Market Street, Suite 400
Philadelphia, PA 19106, USA

www.jkp.com

Copyright © Midori Ochiai, Shinya Miyamoto and Hiroko Fujiwara 2003
English translation copyright © Esther Sanders 2006

Library of Congress Cataloging in Publication Data

Ochiai, Midori.
    [Jûunin toiro na kaeru no ko. English]
    Different croaks for different folks : all about children with special learning needs / Midori Ochiai with notes
on developmental differences by Shinya Miyamoto ; illustrated by Hiroko Fujiwara ; translated by Esther Sanders.
        p. cm.
    ISBN-13: 978-1-84310-392-9 (hardcover)
    ISBN-10: 1-84310-392-3 (hardcover)
    1. Learning disabled children—Life skills guides. 2. Learning disabled children—Popular works. 3. Learning
disabled children—Education. 4. Developmentally disabled children—Life skills guides. 5. Developmentally disabled
children—Popular works. 6. Developmentally disabled children—Education. I. Title.
    RJ506.L4O3413 2006
    618.92'85889—dc22

                                                                                    2005018188

British Library Cataloguing in Publication Data
A CIP catalogue record for this book is available from the British Library

ISBN-13: 978 1 84310 392 9
ISBN-10: 1 84310 392 3

Printed and bound in the People's Republic of China
APC-FT3927

Contents

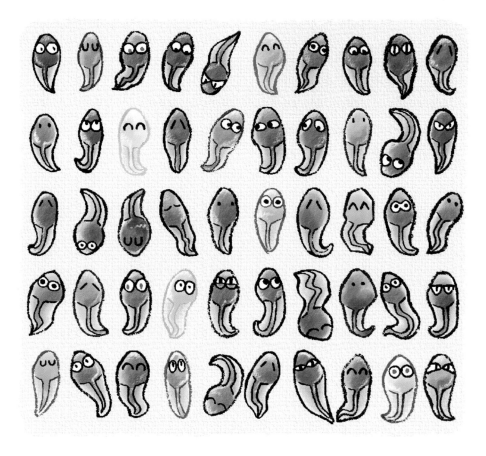

Look at all those tadpoles! They seem very similar, but look very closely. Each one is a little bit different from all the others. And each one will grow at its own pace. What one finds easy might be very hard for another.

You've probably heard that when tadpoles get hands and feet they become frogs. When they're young, frog boys and girls still have their tadpole tails. Let's talk about some of these frog children.

Oh, no! There's a frog falling off a leaf! What's wrong?

What?! He says he doesn't know how to make his body move the way he wants it to. They're his own hands and feet, but he can't get them to do what they're supposed to.

8

Not only that, he also has trouble imitating the other frog children.

Poor frog! He's having trouble telling left from right, up from down, where one thing ends and another begins. Different sounds all get jumbled together, and he finds it hard to figure out where each sound is coming from. He's really having a hard time!

Even though his ears can hear, it's hard for him to learn words because the sounds get all mixed up.

Even though his eyes can see, it's hard for him to learn what things are because everything looks like a mishmash.

When it comes to learning how to read, you can bet he's in for a tough time!

And when it comes to learning how to count and do arithmetic, you know he's bound to have a rough ride, too!

Here are some bright ideas!

We can give the frog a chance to practice on something easy, like a ladder, before he has to climb a leaf. This will help him get used to using his feet.

Our frog friend is certainly trying hard enough. He's not lazy when it comes to studying. What's more, he really *can* learn. But he needs to learn things in a different way from the other frog boys and girls.

So if someone will just show him a way to learn things that suits his style, he'll do a much better job!

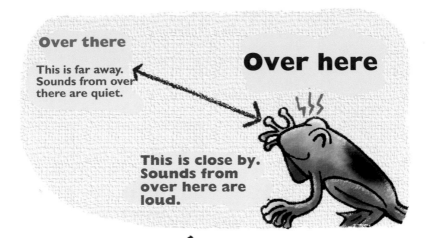

We can give him hints about how to listen...

...and about where to look, so he can figure things out.

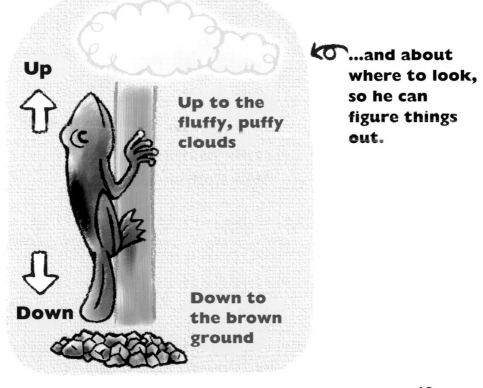

13

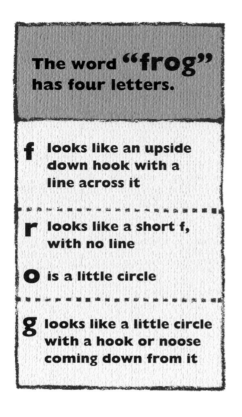

The word "frog" has four letters.

f looks like an upside down hook with a line across it

r looks like a short f, with no line

o is a little circle

g looks like a little circle with a hook or noose coming down from it

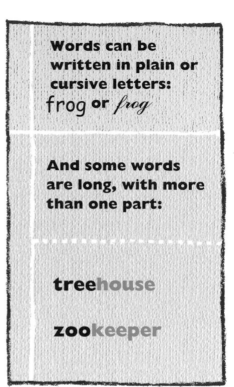

Words can be written in plain or cursive letters:
frog **or** *frog*

And some words are long, with more than one part:

treehouse

zookeeper

What's behind all this trouble he's having with learning words? And with doing arithmetic?

If we think hard about it, we can find lots of little tricks to make things easier.

This shape represents a frog:

This shape represents a leaf:

When we want to compare how many of each there are,

1   2   3

we can try putting one set of shapes above the other.

Learning is like going up a staircase. Some kids run straight to the top, but others take it slowly, one step at a time. It's really nice when these children have someone to walk with them, side by side, and teach them what they need to know.

Teacher Toad's Special Lesson No. 2

For Children with Hard-to-break Habits

What's going on?!

Uh oh! This little brown frog girl is sitting on a green leaf. She needs to change her color to match the leaf, or else a snake might find her and eat her! But when grown-ups tell her this, it seems as if she can't even hear them.

But it's not that she can't hear. And she's not just being stubborn or standoffish either. She doesn't know how to make her body change color to match her surroundings. She also doesn't understand that being a different color from the leaf makes her stick out.

Wait. I'll give her a new leaf that matches the color of her body. There. That's much safer, right?

First, we need to help her so she feels safe coming down from the green leaf.

Then we can give her a
brown leaf instead.

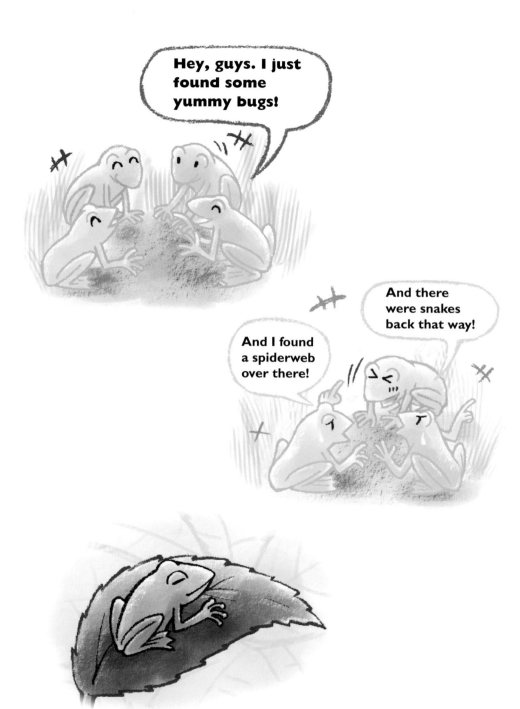

This little frog girl just sits on her leaf all day, listening to the other children talking. They've tried inviting her to join them, but she won't budge.

Lately, they've given up and don't want to be her friend anymore.

It's not that she dislikes the other children, or that she's too shy to speak up. The fact is, she just doesn't know what she's supposed to do. There are lots and lots of things about how to be a kid that she hasn't figured out yet.

So Teacher Toad has drawn her a picture.

It might seem like all frogs are supposed to just know this stuff without needing a picture. But this frog feels scared when she doesn't know ahead of time what a place looks like, or exactly where things (like snakes and spiders) are, or what might happen where.

It really helps her when a grown-up takes the time to show her.

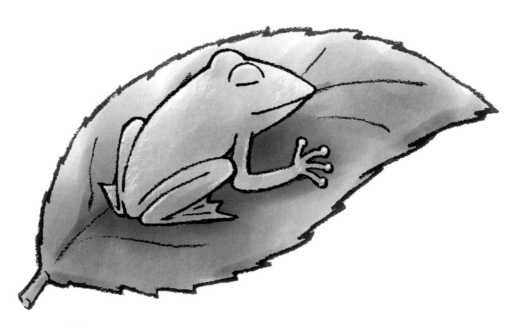

Hey, look! She's come down from her leaf. She'll do even better out here if there are signs to remind her of what she learned from Teacher Toad's picture.

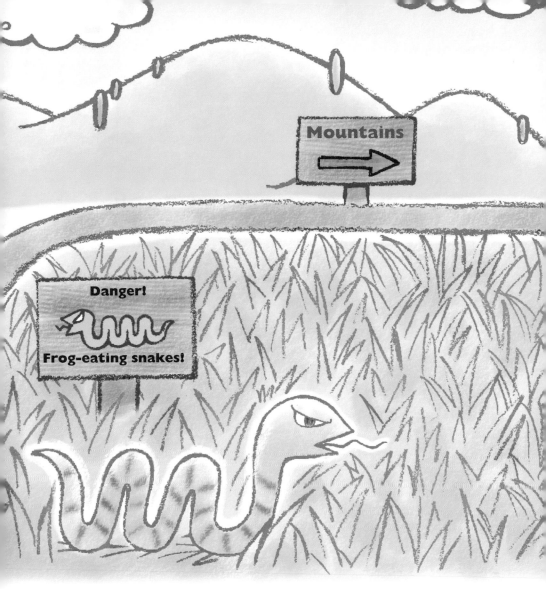

Oh, yes, and don't forget the travel-sized leaf. She doesn't actually need it for protection, but just having it with her makes her feel very safe, and that's important!

**Teacher Toad's
Special Lesson
No. 3**
For Children Who Have
Problems Socializing

Uh oh! This little frog boy is talking non-stop to poor Mr. Bullfrog.

I know he just wants to be friendly, but Mr. Bullfrog can't listen to so much chatter all at once.

Why do you have spots?

Do you eat crayfish?

You look really cool when you're swimming!

What's your name?

We're friends, right?

You're fat!

When is your birthday?

You have big ears! I bet you hear really well!

Are you related to leopard frogs?

Have you ever heard of poison dart frogs?

Exhausted

How's it going?

Are you tired?

Come on!
Play with me!

Now the little frog boy has gone back again to visit
Mr. Bullfrog, who looks exhausted! But the little
frog boy keeps trying to get Mr. Bullfrog to talk and
play with him.

This makes Mr. Bullfrog angry. But the little frog
boy doesn't understand why, so he gets angry too.

What the little boy frog needs is a lesson like this:

I'm angry

It hurts

I'm disappointed

Grown-ups often say that we can see people's feelings on their faces, but for this little frog boy it's very, very hard!

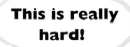

He just can't seem to figure out what people are feeling by looking at them.

Two people can have different feelings at the same time

Here's an important lesson for you to learn: you and the person you're with might not always feel the same way at the same time even if you're friends.

So just because you're having fun, it doesn't mean that your friend is also having fun. And he or she might not get angry at the same things that make you angry.

When people talk to each other, it's important to use good manner phrases, like "Can we talk now?", "Thank you!" and "I'm sorry!" These words will help both you and the person you're talking to feel good.

And there are also other rules of conversation that will help you and your friends enjoy each other's company.

Teacher Toad's Special Lesson No. 4

For Children Who Are Easily Distracted

This little frog girl is always getting interested in too many things all at the same time. Sometimes she even forgets what she was just getting ready to do. She starts projects and then leaves them halfway through without finishing them. She also loses the things she's supposed to have with her. She even loses the special treasures she was trying so hard to take good care of! Grown-ups are always getting angry with her for being careless.

Even when she is sad over losing something she loves, grown-ups still scold her, and this makes her feel even sadder. It would be better if parents and teachers used more gentle words to teach her. Instead of saying "You need to be more careful!", they could say, "I think there's something different you're supposed to be doing right now," or "Aren't you forgetting something?"

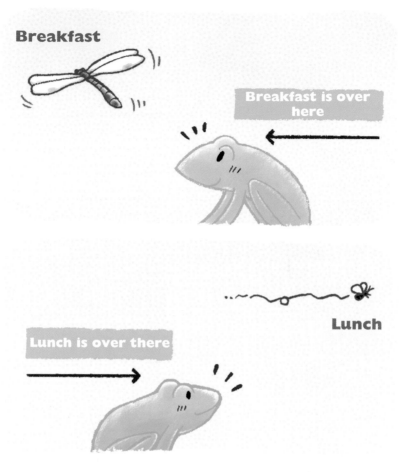

Breakfast

Breakfast is over here

Lunch

Lunch is over there

Now the little frog girl is really trying her best and thinking, "This time I'm going to do it right!" But if there are too many things to look at all at once, she'll get confused. A helpful grown-up has put away all the extra things that were distracting her. And every time she finishes something, the grown-up tells her, "Good job!" This makes her very, very happy.

This frog girl has trouble remembering to do what she's supposed to and loses interest after just a few minutes. So the best way for her to get things done is to start promptly, before she forgets, and finish quickly, before she gets bored.

Teacher Toad's Special Lesson No. 5

For Children Who Get Obsessed with Their Hobbies

No!

Look out!

It's great to be so interested in something that nothing else distracts you. But you can also get into serious trouble. Like this frog boy, who might get eaten by a bird or a snake if he doesn't pay attention!

This frog boy loves bugs!

When you enjoy something, you want to keep doing it forever, right? Some children love their hobbies so much that it seems like they know everything about them. When they grow up, they may even become professors!

When you're doing something you really like non-stop, do grown-ups ever say, "Don't you know there are lots more important things you should be doing?!"

It's good to know a lot, but it's not OK to talk about it anytime you feel like it. You need to be careful not to interrupt people when they're busy.

You may even get to be a world-famous expert someday doing for a living what you love the most.

But remember: There are rules you need to follow!

What's the problem here? This frog boy seems to be misunderstanding his friend.

Your personal space

OK, here's what the problem is: This frog boy doesn't leave enough space between himself and other people for everyone to move around safely. Then when he bumps into his friends by accident, he doesn't realize it was his fault, so he hits them. This just gets him in worse trouble.

Your friend's personal space

Stretch out your arms and pretend there's a bubble around you that's *this* wide.

But there's a simple trick that can help him understand how to keep his distance: He can imagine that he and his friends are all surrounded by large "safety bubbles" filled with air.

Counting slowly from one to ten in your mind will help you turn...

...from hot red...   **...to cool blue!**

And he can also practice the famous "count to ten" trick to use whenever he starts to feel too angry.

No, you just have a bad habit, that's all.

So it's important for you to learn what to do instead.

I'm a bad boy!

This trick is a way of helping yourself relax and get control of your feelings.

OK, everyone.

Let's put this all together.

Work with me here: You've just been reading a bunch of stories about young frogs who have an unusual way of doing things and sometimes cause trouble to their friends, parents, and teachers. You could say that these frog children have a different sort of "croak" from typical folk.

Now pay close attention. Who do you think feels worse about the trouble that gets caused, the unusual frogs, or everyone else?

Good for you if you guessed that it's the unusual frogs; you're with me!

Tadpoles can't climb trees...

...or walk across the ground.

Try to remember how it felt to be a tiny infant still in diapers, or a toddler. There's no such thing as a newborn child—whether human or amphibian— who knows how to do the things that most older

And they can't catch bugs...

...or jump in the cool way their parents do...

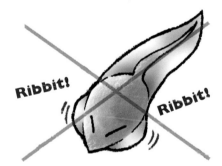

Ribbit!

Ribbit!

...or say what's on their minds.

kids and grown-ups take for granted. Every one of us learned what we know now gradually, one step at a time.

There are all

Some are big, some are small.
No two look exactly alike.
Some like to follow behind.

Some like to spin
in circles.

Some do the opposite
of everyone else, and
others just go their
own way.

Some like to
zig-zag.

Some prefer to sit
still and observe.

Some are always clinging
to their favorite things.

kinds of babies:

Some get scared easily and make a big fuss.

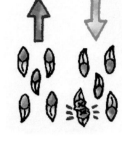

Some just can't seem to follow the rules.

Some lose their tempers a lot.

Some don't talk or make any sound at all.

Some prefer to play by themselves.

Some are a little bit clumsy.

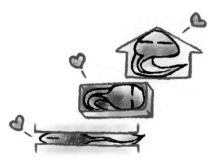

And some love squeezing themselves into tight spaces.

When it comes to babies, nobody minds any of their little quirks and unusual habits. So why is it that when they get older and start school, all of a sudden being "different" becomes a major issue?

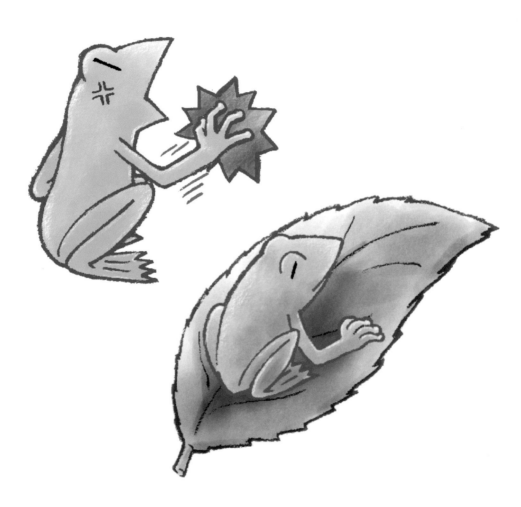

Today's lecture:
Poisonous beetles

May cause symptoms of peripheral neuropathy when eaten. Found near wet, grassy areas...

Prof. T.S. Pinkum

Think about all the grown-ups you know. They all have different kinds of jobs, and different things that they're good at and not good at.

There's nothing wrong with variety! In fact, the world is an interesting place precisely because there are so many different kinds of people.

Just as everyone's
face is unique,
everyone also has a unique
way of doing things.
We all have our own
special, wonderful way
of being.

We all have the right to take our time and grow in our own way.

There's no rush!

There are children in the world who have a special way of learning things. And that is perfectly OK.

A Message to Children

This book, especially the illustrated main section, was written both for children and grown-ups. If you are a child reading this, then perhaps you looked at one or more of the frogs and thought to yourself, "That's just like me!" (Did you?) If you think you are, like the frogs, a bit "different" from most other people your age, then the first thing you should do is to get a clear understanding of your own special differences. Once you have this understanding, it will be much easier to figure out what you should do next.

The frogs in this book are examples of just a few of the different types of children in the world. There are many other examples as well, because there are many ways of being unusual. And there are also many people who can give you help and encouragement when you are feeling bad about yourself or when your differences are causing you problems. I hope you will let these people work with you so that you can find ways of doing things that work for you.

Here are some good mottoes to remember:

 It's OK to be different!

 There's no gain in blame! (Some problems are just not anyone's fault.)

 Start with what you can do, not with what you can't do!

Explanatory Notes on Special Needs for Parents and Caregivers

Special needs in general

While tadpoles of course have much in common with frogs, their appearance at birth is decidedly unfroglike. Tadpoles breathe through gills and can live only in water. Eventually, they sprout legs, then arms, and gradually they change color. And then one day, they begin breathing through lungs and leave the water.

But human children come into the world already looking, well, human. Because their general shape gives children the appearance of being more or less like us, the adults, it's easy for us to take their growth for granted, to see their maturing as a simple, linear process: One day older, one day closer to being adults. In an important sense, though, children are no different from tadpoles. Their shapes may remain essentially the same, but the process they must go through to reach adulthood is no less complex and spectacular than that of a tadpole transforming into a frog.

A newborn baby cannot independently fulfill even the most basic needs of survival, such as obtaining food or maintaining its own body temperature. Neither can it move from place to place nor take care of expelled waste. Infants depend on their parents or other adult caregivers for almost everything required for sustaining life itself, not to mention protection from physical harm.

As time passes, the tiny individual who at first spent most of its time sleeping learns to support the considerable weight of its own head, and then goes on to master crawling and walking. As the child acquires vocabulary and the ability to converse, he or she gains knowledge of and access to the world with astonishing speed. At this stage, even small concerns may be a source of great anxiety for parents, who are often told not to worry, that it is perfectly natural for young children to develop skills at an uneven pace. And, in fact, the range of ability considered "normal" for any given skill tends to be fairly wide to begin with.

Nevertheless, studies have revealed that some 6 to 7 percent of all children show paths of development that are starkly different from those seen in most of their age-mates. These children have what are sometimes referred to as developmental "disorders," a term that conjures up images of something quite severe. A more apt term is "hurdles." An obstacle course, despite its ups and downs, can still be traversed. This is similar to the development of some children whose particular challenge it is to surmount a variety of hurdles as they grow.

A few of these children have visible differences, but most do not. More importantly, all these children are engaged in a continual process of development and in this way are no different from any other children. By no means do they merely stand still.

They seem to walk a different road from other children, and at times they come upon hurdles that appear to bar their way completely. But viewed from a different angle, these hurdles can be seen as highly unusual characteristics that confer upon these children unique patterns of growth.

The section that follows discusses how these principles apply to the types of children characterized in this book—the frogs who "croak differently" from their peers. For ease of understanding, I have used each character to represent only one developmental difficulty, but in fact it is common for affected children to have multiple difficulties. Moreover, I would like to encourage readers to see development as a lifelong process rather than—as is commonly thought—a process that occurs only during childhood.

Special learning needs in particular

Refer to "Teacher Toad's Special Lesson No. 1: For Children with Uneven Development" on page 8 and also to the sections in the notes on developmental differences concerning learning disabilities (page 91), developmental coordination disorder (page 91), and developmental language disorder (page 92).

At school, all children are ordinarily expected to study the same subjects in the same way. This standardized instruction is geared to the needs of the majority of children, but there are invariably some students who find it too easy, while others find it too difficult in the sense that it is unsuited to their own style of learning. In most of the latter cases, the difficulties encountered fall within a range that can be considered ordinary variances in skill level, but there are always a few children who stand out as having learning needs that are special.

For example, running or simply moving one's limbs are activities that come naturally to most children. Contrast this with children who, left to their own devices, do not learn to use their arms and legs with ease and cannot imitate the movements of others or figure out how to "go with the flow" of what is happening around them. This is one example of a developmental hurdle.

Some children who cannot yet read or write face different hurdles. For example, they may be unable to distinguish up from down and left from right. They may have trouble learning the names of different objects because of an inability to visually discriminate between the objects themselves. They may perceive distinct sounds as though they were all jumbled together. Or, at a given moment, they may be unable to separate the main stimulus that requires their attention (a sound or a shape, for example) from all the other stimuli in the background.

Another category of hurdles concerns numbers: counting them, adding them, comparing them, and so on. Children who experience such difficulties will struggle with even the simplest arithmetic, let alone mathematical procedures such as carrying or unit conversion.

These children, contrary to superficial appearances, are not lazy, slacking off, or merely avoiding subjects they dislike. They have trouble learning and need to be taught in special ways that are tailored to their individual needs. And sometimes parents and teachers need to change their ways of thinking, allowing that it might be better for the child to use a word processor or a calculator instead of struggling in vain with penmanship or math; in some cases this change in attitude may be more productive than the anxious, dead-end thinking that the child simply must somehow learn to write, compute prices or change, and so on in order to avoid problems in later life.

Visual or auditory difficulties can be lifelong, so it is best to think in terms of encouraging children toward careers where these issues will be less conspicuous. There are many adults who attest to having had learning problems involving sensory dysfunctions when they were children. Celebrities such as Tom Cruise, who has publicly acknowledged having grown up with dyslexia, have cast the individuality and potential of people with learning difficulties in a positive light.

Some individuals have grown up with academic difficulties and then gained recognition in the public eye as actors and models, but also in careers such as professional sports, perhaps because of some exceptional quality. Yet, one often hears that as children they were ashamed of the very quality that led to their success. Traits that they despised when younger became prized assets to them in adulthood. The same applies to hidden qualities such as differences in visual perception or in thought patterns. These unusual characteristics may put children at a disadvantage during their school years, but they should also be seen as special talents that may later become the driving force behind unique professional achievement. There is no reason whatsoever why everyone must proceed along the same career path.

Special ways of interacting

Refer to "Teacher Toad's Special Lesson No. 2: For Children with Hard-to-break Habits" (page 16) and "Teacher Toad's Special Lesson No. 3: For Children Who Have Problems Socializing" (page 26) and also to the section in the notes on developmental differences concerning pervasive developmental disorders (page 83).

Certain types of children don't make a very good impression on the people around them, because they behave in ways that are associated with being ill-mannered. The problems they experience are many and varied, but here are a few examples: having difficulty "playing nicely" with other children; exhibiting odd gestures or facial expressions; using peculiar figures of speech; having difficulty making wishes understood, or understanding the wishes of others; blithely doing things that are generally considered embarrassing; or behaving in ways that indicate a lack of understanding of other people's feelings, such as tagging along with others persistently, even when they give clear signals of wanting to be left alone.

The reasons for these behaviors are also many and varied. Children who act this way may have trouble adjusting to the situation around them; they may be generally and extremely fearful such that any little thing might cause them to shrink or lose control; they may simply have fallen into a pattern of unusual habits; or they may be unable to engage in activities that involve give-and-take.

In the past, most such children were thought to have delayed speech, but it is now understood that many affected children have deficits in communication and socialization even in the absence of speech delays.

These children can be helped if the supervising adults are willing to apply the following guidelines:

1. Don't pressure the child into doing what everyone else is doing. As a first step, try adjusting to his or her needs.

2. Make sure you have a place set aside where the child can go to feel secure. Let the child know that this is a

place where he or she can act naturally and will not be disturbed.

3. If the child is making eccentric gestures or other movements, just stand by and watch. Consider the possibility that this behavior is helping the child gain a sense of security, or that it may simply be a source of enjoyment. At the same time, be aware that when odd gesturing or movement suddenly becomes very pronounced, this may be a sign of stress.

4. When the child has a tantrum or "meltdown," take the position that he or she has, in fact, experienced something perceived as loathsome or frightening. Adopting this perspective will help you understand the reason behind the child's behavior.

5. Adjust the child's environment to remove as many anxiety-provoking elements as possible. This should help to prevent problem behaviors in the first place.

In order to better understand these children's feelings, imagine that you are alone in a foreign country and do not speak or understand the language. Consider how ecstatic you would be if suddenly, somehow, you could communicate and make yourself understood. If you are the parent of or look after such a child, do become someone who can impart a sense of security to that child. The more such adults there are in the child's environment, the more he or she will be able to settle down and behave appropriately.

It is generally assumed that playing and talking with friends is something that comes naturally and that all children enjoy, but the children described here have their own unusual way of thinking and feeling. As a result, they have unique ways of enjoying themselves, and, conversely, will often be extremely distressed over things that would matter little or not at all to most people. This is not to say that they dislike everyone around them. They, too, want to participate with others, but they need to participate differently.

Among children who have social difficulties, some have trouble interacting at all, while others enthusiastically seek out opportunities to do so. These two types of children give very different impressions from one another, but they have one fundamental trait in common: an inability to adjust their behavior to suit the different situations they find themselves in. It is important to be aware that symptoms of social difficulty can vary widely from one child to another.

In particular, they are often at a loss for how to behave, and may become very upset when faced with situations where a subtle understanding of etiquette is required. They may not understand, for example, that an individual's feelings can change from one occasion to another and that in such cases—depending on the nature of their relationship to the other person—they may be expected to accommodate that person by adjusting their own attitude.

Having said all this, though, it must be added that there is of course a limit to the extent to which others should adjust to the needs of children who face these types of problems. No man is an island, and if these youngsters do not learn how to get along in the world, then it is the children who will eventually suffer. It is also very important that they learn skills with which to forge and strengthen relationships so that they do not end up living in isolation, being shunned, or engaging in antisocial behavior.

Children who have trouble picking up social cues from their environment can be helped with special instructions. Pictures, or carefully chosen words, can be used to explain to a child in very specific and easily understandable terms, "This is what people may do here," or "These are the things that you may do now." The purpose of such instructions is to impart skills that will eventually help these children to function independently in society.

Other educational interventions include teaching children explicitly how to interpret people's feelings based on their facial expressions and teaching detailed rules for how to have a conversation. It is important to not only present fixed rules for children to learn by rote, but also to premise this training on the idea that each person has individual thoughts and feelings; it may be necessary to wait until the child has gained awareness of this principle before introducing this type of training.

Simultaneously, instructions should be given to the child's peers to help them understand that there are people who have unusual ways of thinking and feeling. This dual effort will help close the gap between typical children and those affected by social difficulties. This method is preferable to pointing the finger and accusing a child of being insensitive to other people's feelings, without any effort to make helpful suggestions.

Trouble with attention and self-control

Refer to "Teacher Toad's Special Lesson No. 4: For Children Who Are Easily Distracted" (page 36), "Teacher Toad's Special Lesson No. 5: For Children Who Get Obsessed with Their Hobbies" (page 40), and "Teacher Toad's Special Lesson No. 6: For Children Who Jump to Conclusions" (page 46) and also to the section in the notes on developmental differences concerning attention deficit hyperactivity disorder (page 89).

There seem to be lots and lots of children who are easily distracted. We're always hearing about kids who "can't concentrate" or "don't get their acts together." How do we then distinguish ordinary distractibility from something that represents a genuine developmental hurdle? In the latter case, the affected child will tend to start many projects but leave them all unfinished; sometimes, confusion may reign to the extent that the child suddenly forgets what he or she was right in the middle of doing.

The period of time during which such a child can attend to a single task is extremely short. His or her eyes may dart from one object to another, and it may be a huge struggle to filter out background noise and discriminate the one sound requiring immediate attention.

In order to help the child, we must reduce or eliminate extraneous information and organize the environment so that it is very clear to the child what he or she is supposed to be doing. The child should not be expected to try to do more than one thing at a time, and items needed for an upcoming task should be kept out of sight while the current task is being worked on.

Adults should also resign themselves to the fact that brevity of attention span will not simply go away with training; forgetfulness, therefore, should be considered par for the course and responded to with gentle instruction rather than scolding. Conversely, when such a child does manage to remember even something minor, he or she should be praised to the skies!

As the child grows, his or her attention span will gradually increase. But even more powerful than the effect of time is praise. Words of encouragement will build the child's confidence and go a long way toward cultivating both self-acceptance and self-motivation. This is because children who face this particular hurdle also tend to be especially apprehensive about being scolded and prone to losing their motivation.

It is perfectly natural for anyone to lose track of time when having fun or when absorbed in a favorite activity. We all prefer to spend our time doing things we enjoy, and there is certainly nothing wrong with becoming an expert at one's favorite subject. As the famous artist and poet John Ruskin said, "When love and skill work together, expect a masterpiece." Having interests and talents is generally a good thing. But when these are pursued to an unreasonable extreme, they should be regarded as a developmental hurdle.

There are, for example, children who will choose an activity and become so deeply absorbed in it that they are utterly unable to attend to routine personal care or follow the ordinary rhythm of daily life. These children may be a storehouse of sophisticated knowledge, but they cannot dress themselves. This type of child is often mistakenly thought of as selfish or lazy.

Not only that, but the child may actively annoy others by chattering endlessly about his or her subject of interest—anytime, anywhere, and with no participation whatsoever in the activity or discussion that others are engaged in. At least, such children need to be taught to follow prearranged cues based on common sense and generally accepted etiquette, indicating when they may start talking and when they should stop.

Timers and alarm clocks, if used judiciously, can also give effective help to children who tend to get "lost" in their activities or have trouble making the transition from one activity to another.

The ability to become deeply absorbed and the possession of a conspicuous talent are wonderful assets. Parents and teachers should give children with attention and self-control problems positive guidance and encouragement and help them to keep sight of their own genuine worth. The assets that one sees in them now may eventually prove to be the basis for the acquisition of professional expertise or certification in some field or other, and this is certainly a desirable outcome.

There is also the matter of some children being "high-strung." It's good to be energetic, but some children can get rowdy or aggressive and then suddenly begin sulking. This behavior pattern can sometimes occur because the child has misunderstood the intentions of another person. Thus, a child bumped into by accident may think he or she has been deliberately struck, or a child standing right in the middle of the hallway may wonder why he or she keeps getting "purposely" shoved.

Adults witnessing outbursts in situations like these should not make judgments based solely on the behavior that meets the eye. Claims of "misunderstanding" may ring false, but in fact they are all too true. It is therefore useless to expect scolding or preaching about morals to solve the problem. Even when these children understand appropriate rules of behavior, they face a developmental hurdle characterized by poor self-control and difficulty putting their knowledge and understanding into practice. Your goal should not be merely to teach them to apologize, but also to help them develop the skill of acting on what they know.

There are also children who have difficulty thinking things through. With these children, it is important to confirm in each instance of inappropriate behavior whether or not they actually understand the applicable rules of right and wrong and to review these rules if necessary.

In this book, the example of a child not keeping an appropriate distance from others has been used. A problem like this will never be solved with a general instruction such as "You need to leave more space." The child will have a much easier time learning with concrete visual aids, such as a large ball or a hula hoop, and by actually observing how much space is required for one's arms and legs to move freely.

In addition, children who tend to misconstrue others' intentions are often helped when picture cards, role-play, and so on are used to teach the meanings implicit in certain kinds of movements and to provide practice at interpreting different types of social encounters. It is also important to supplement this training with practice at self-control so that the child can learn to avoid flying into a rage when problems do occur.

A few final words

It's only natural to feel embarrassed about not being as good at something as other people, or as good as one "should" be for one's age. Ability is of course a good thing, and without the desire to strive, there would be no self-improvement. But does this also mean that inability is a bad thing?

First, bear in mind that the abilities we usually take for granted and expect to see in others are merely a reflection of what happens to be true for the majority. When someone gets angry at another person's lack of competence in a certain skill, this seems the same as saying, "I expect you to be able to do whatever I can do" and finding it intolerable when this expectation is not met.

And so, if ever you find yourself distressed about your son, daughter, or student being a "problem child," remember this:

„ The one who faces the biggest problem and feels the greatest distress is the child, not you or anyone else.

„ You can help the child by working together to think of ideas that will make things easier or less stressful for him or her.

„ This kind of help does not entail trying to make differences disappear. It's important to accept the differences as a given and to focus on helping the child to reduce problems and to cope effectively when problems do arise.

Notes on Developmental Differences

Shinya Miyamoto, Institute of Disabilities Science, University of Tsukuba

The illustrated section of this book presents information about developmental hurdles in a very user-friendly manner. Below, this presentation is supplemented with an introduction to the relevant medical concepts and terminology. The discussion has deliberately been kept as simple as possible; readers who wish to study the subject in greater depth are encouraged to take advantage of the many excellent resources available both in print and online.

Developmental disorders
What are developmental disorders?

A developmental disorder is defined as a serious delay in the development of adaptive, cognitive, and/or social skills that appears anytime before the age of 18. It often affects higher cortical function, which refers to processes that involve multiple parts of the brain and allow us to carry out all of the complicated mental work associated with being human: speaking, comprehending when spoken to, thinking, and so on. In contrast to these complex processes, some functions—such as vision, hearing, and movement of the limbs—are carried out by only one section of the brain. Therefore, for example, a child who is born visually impaired because of dysfunction involving the visual cortex (located at the back of the brain) would not be considered to have a developmental disorder.

Medical professionals generally divide developmental disorders into four categories: (1) cognitive developmental disorders, characterized mainly by intellectual deficits (e.g., a low IQ); (2) pervasive developmental disorders (also known as autistic spectrum disorders); (3) attention deficit hyperactivity disorder; and (4) specific disorders of a more limited nature, such as speech impairments or motor skills deficits. Thus, when a child is evaluated for a developmental disorder, the clinician first determines into which of these four categories the child's problems fall.

"Mild" developmental disorders

When a developmental disorder is classified as "mild," it simply means that the disorder does not involve an impairment of cognitive functioning, not that the symptoms themselves are necessarily mild. "No impairment in cognitive functioning" can mean one of two things, and the distinction is purely technical: (1) the child has an IQ of 70 or higher and is therefore not intellectually disabled, or (2) the child has an IQ of 85 or higher and therefore has full intellectual ability in the normal range. IQs of 71–84 are, by definition, considered "borderline." In recent years, the second definition has come to be more widely accepted than the first. The term "mild," used in this sense, is more or less synonymous with the term "high-functioning," which is discussed below.

When talking about developmental disorders in children with normal intelligence, the specific conditions referred to include high-functioning autism and Asperger's syndrome, disorders in specific areas of development, and attention deficit hyperactivity disorder. Often, however, children with borderline intelligence or mild intellectual disability (IQs of 50–70) are loosely grouped in this category; this is because they experience many of the same problems and often need precisely the same kinds of special considerations as children who, by the above definition, have mild developmental disorders.

Individual disorders
Pervasive developmental disorders
What are pervasive developmental disorders?

Since the 1980s, autism and a handful of other disorders resembling autism have come to be classified together. As a group, these conditions are usually referred to as either pervasive developmental disorders (PDDs) or autistic spectrum disorders (ASDs). The latter term is premised on the idea that classic autism, Asperger's syndrome (described below), and related conditions all have fundamental elements in common and that they should therefore be considered part of the same continuum, rather than completely separate disorders. Throughout this section, I will be using the term PDD.

Among the conditions that fall under the PDD umbrella are classic autism (generally severe), high-functioning autism, atypical autism, and Asperger's syndrome (less severe and characterized by the absence of intellectual impairments and delays in the development of speech).

PDDs are defined by four characteristics: (1) difficulty engaging in social interaction with others; (2) difficulty using and understanding all the usual modes of communication (speech, gestures, facial expressions, and so on); (3) difficulties related to imagination; and (4) a strong tendency for activities and interests to be restricted to a narrow range. Whenever all four of these characteristics are observed, the child who displays them is said to have a pervasive developmental disorder.

The prevalence of autism

Researchers currently believe that the prevalence of autism is about one to two individuals per 1000 (0.1%–0.2%). Autism is three to four times more common among boys than among girls. This is in part because the male brain is generally more fragile and prone to illness or injury than the female brain. Experts are not yet certain of what causes autism, but it is now understood that the condition results from some sort of problem with the brain itself and not from anything inadequate or inappropriate in parenting techniques or the child's environment.

The four basic characteristics of autism and other PDDs

DIFFICULTY WITH SOCIAL INTERACTION

Individuals with autism tend to interact with others in a one-sided manner, without the normal give-and-take that most people expect. In young children, more specific symptoms include difficulty with eye contact, a tendency not to turn when one's name is called, an absence of stranger anxiety, and an absence of finger-pointing. After early childhood, the following other characteristics often emerge: an inability to share enjoyment with others, difficulty making friends, and an inability to interpret clues indicative of other people's emotions and circumstances.

It is important to understand that autism rarely entails the stereotypical profile of a person closed off in his or her own world, shunning any and all contact with others. On the contrary, some autistic individuals will warm to others with no reservations whatsoever and give the superficial appearance of being extremely affable. But even in these cases the person with autism is likely to interact in a way that lacks reciprocity, for example speaking much and listening very little, if at all.

DIFFICULTY WITH COMMUNICATION

Children with autism encounter a number of difficulties related to producing and comprehending speech, and they often have a peculiar way of talking. They may talk out loud to themselves, have trouble making conversation, and frequently change the subject in an unnatural way. They may also tend to parrot back what they hear; this is called echolalia. Echolalia often occurs when a child lacks comprehension and therefore will tend to decrease as he or she becomes more advanced at understanding spoken language. There is often an unnatural quality to the child's voice, with monotone and slightly high-pitched speech being common, as is the tendency to end words or sentences with a rising tone. Because of these unusual mannerisms, there are occasionally children with autism who lack the regional accents of the locations in which they live.

DIFFICULTIES RELATED TO IMAGINATION

Young autistic children tend to have difficulty mentally picturing things that are not physically present in front of them, or imagining hypothetical or fantastical situations. As a result, they tend not to engage in pretend play and instead repeat the same simple games over and over. As they get older, they tend to have trouble with abstract concepts and symbolic imagery and have difficulty understanding the meanings of words that do not have specific, concrete referents—for example, words that denote categories of objects (such as "animal," "fruit," etc.), adverbs, adjectives, and so on.

Because of their difficulty comprehending things that are not explicitly stated or shown, children with autism tend to be unaware of many unwritten rules of behavior and of the so-called common sense or common knowledge that most children absorb without any direct teaching.

RESTRICTED ACTIVITIES AND INTERESTS
Children with autism often have fixed and limited areas of interest, for example letters, numbers, or product brand names. In addition, they usually lack flexibility and may become tense or upset when something does not go as planned or is not done in the usual or preferred way.

Other cognitive and behavioral characteristics

Children with autism often have difficulty making inferences and may therefore not understand speech where relevant words have been left out because the speaker considers them obvious. For example, picture a father and a son who has autism in a restaurant, menus in hand. Dad asks, "What looks good to you?" and receives the unexpected reply, "Soccer uniforms!" A more helpful way for the father to phrase his question would have been to ask, "What would you like to eat?" Other issues in this category include trouble with pronouns (because the objects or people they refer to change from one situation to the next) and a tendency to interpret words literally, so that the point of humor or sarcasm is frequently missed.

Another common characteristic of autism is "face blindness," or difficulty distinguishing people's faces. Children with this characteristic struggle even to remember the faces and names of their classmates. And in the weeks or months that it takes them to assimilate this information, they are unable to associate specific acts of kindness (or unkindness) with the individuals who committed them; this makes them prone to misunderstandings and to being perceived as cold or perfunctory in the way they treat people.

Physiological characteristics

Approximately 50 percent of children with autism show abnormal electrical activity in the brain (abnormal "brain waves") when given electroencephalograms (EEGs). About 20 percent experience seizures. Both seizures and abnormal EEGs tend to appear for the first time after age ten, so children who have been diagnosed with autism or a related condition should undergo EEG testing at regular intervals until roughly age 15 to 18.

Sleep disturbances are also common and are likely to be caused by a dysfunction in the part of the brain that regulates the circadian rhythm. One common pattern is that of nighttime wakefulness, which lasts for approximately one to three months and then disappears spontaneously.

Finally, extreme motor clumsiness is another common characteristic of children with autism. (See also the section below on developmental coordination disorder.)

High-functioning PDDs

As mentioned earlier, "high-functioning" is defined simply as the absence of intellectual impairment (i.e., having an IQ that is near-normal or above). Broadly speaking, the two types of high-functioning PDD are high-functioning autism (characterized by deficits or delays in speech) and Asperger's syndrome (characterized by the absence of such deficits or delays). Children who have one of these conditions tend to function comparably well when interacting one-on-one, and they are usually capable of participating in certain group activities that are highly structured. Trouble often arises in group social situations involving play or other interaction that is unstructured. Other features seen in these children include tendencies to speak and act at their own pace, seemingly without regard for the feelings and circumstances of the people they are with; to speak in a one-sided manner on topics of personal interest; to interpret words literally without comprehending implicit meanings; to lack flexibility in thinking or behavior; to engage in compulsive behavior and be very insistent on having things a certain way; and to speak or behave in ways that may be annoying or harmful to others.

Until recently, many children with high-functioning PDDs were consigned to being on the receiving end of constant criticism for being "selfish" or "willful," while their parents were blamed for incompetent childrearing. This situation reflected a lack of general knowledge about the nature of these conditions; children who had normal intelligence and could interact with others to a substantial degree simply were not suspected of having anything that could be called a developmental problem, least of all of having a condition similar to autism.

Attention deficit hyperactivity disorder
What is attention deficit hyperactivity disorder?

This condition, commonly known as ADHD, involves difficulty with paying attention or directing one's attention appropriately and with moderating one's activity or behavior. It includes behavior that is impulsive as well as that which is merely excessive. Broadly speaking the condition is diagnosed when a child has greater difficulty in these areas than would be expected given his or her level of intellectual development.

The prevalence of ADHD

ADHD is thought to occur in about 2 to 3 percent of all children and in roughly three times as many boys as girls. Its causes are not fully understood. In a very small number of cases, symptoms of ADHD appear in children who have experienced abuse or neglect, but these cases are considered to be a separate phenomenon. In fact, the vast majority of children who show symptoms of ADHD have difficulties that are developmental (not environmental) in nature.

Basic characteristics of ADHD
INATTENTION

Children with ADHD often have trouble concentrating their attention to begin a task and tend to be easily distracted from activities they have begun. They often leave projects unfinished, forget to bring the items they need, misplace their belongings, make careless mistakes, and so on. At the same time, they may easily spend hours focused intensely on something they like, such as playing a video game. This, however, should not be confused with genuine concentration, which entails the ability to pay attention when one needs to, not only when one wants to.

HYPERACTIVITY

Hyperactive children are unable to sit still; too frequently, they are either moving about restlessly or else fidgeting or shifting around in their chairs. Adolescents and adults with ADHD sometimes state that they frequently feel emotional tension and have trouble relaxing.

IMPULSIVITY

Children who act impulsively will tend to do something the instant it occurs to them. They have trouble waiting their turn, may cut in front of others instead of standing in line, and may have trouble moderating the intensity of their reactions. When in a group situation, their behavior tends to get them into trouble.

HOW THESE BASIC SYMPTOMS CHANGE OVER TIME

Children with ADHD usually gain self-control naturally as they grow. In situations where at least a minimum of self-control is required, most will be able to keep their hyperactivity within reasonable bounds by about age eight or ten, and their inattention and impulsivity, by about age ten or twelve. But this does not mean that these symptoms have disappeared; rather, it simply means that the child is now able to manage them when necessary. When no such necessity is felt, the child will often continue to exhibit the same extreme behaviors as when he or she was younger.

Learning disabilities

Children who have learning disabilities (LDs) experience great difficulty—despite normal sight, hearing, and overall intelligence—in one or more of the following areas: listening, speaking, reading, writing, calculating, and reasoning. Some children who have one or more LDs also exhibit certain other difficulties, including motor clumsiness, trouble behaving well in groups because of hyperactivity, and inconsistent scores on the various IQ subtests.

One further caveat is necessary: While educators use the acronym LD to stand for "learning disability" as described above, physicians actually use it to stand for "learning disorder." Moreover, physicians limit the definition of learning disorder to include only problems with reading, writing, and calculating. In other words, they exclude difficulties with listening, speaking, and reasoning from their definition of LD. While medical professionals do not have a diagnostic term to refer to problems with reasoning, they include listening and speaking difficulties under the diagnosis developmental language disorder, which is discussed below.

Developmental coordination disorder

This disorder is characterized by a conspicuous lack in the ability to perform everyday tasks requiring motor coordination as compared with the level of skill that would be expected given the child's age or IQ. Motor coordination entails the use of two or more muscle groups working either simultaneously or in succession to perform a set of distinct movements. Skipping, for example, requires that the arms turn the rope while the legs move up and down.

Specific symptoms of developmental coordination disorder include delays in achieving early motor milestones, such as sitting up, crawling, and walking; a tendency to drop things; poor performance at sports and with penmanship; slow and/or awkward movements; and poor balance.

In a substantial number of cases, parents seek consultations because of concern about behavioral problems, and it is then revealed that their children are also experiencing motor difficulties such as those listed above. When clumsiness is impeding a child's ability to function successfully in daily life (and especially in sports or physical education class at school), it is only natural that the child might fall into a state of chronic irritability and become quick-tempered, aggressive, or restless. It is therefore wise for parents worried about their children's behavior to look at motor skills and consider whether difficulty here might not be an underlying cause of stress.

Developmental language disorder

The defining characteristic of this disorder is a delay or deficit in speech that occurs in a child who has normal hearing, intelligence, and social behavior and is being raised in an environment free of any unusual stresses or inadequacies. A diagnosis of developmental language disorder is usually made when a child has not yet begun to say any meaningful words by the age of 18 months, or cannot yet put two or more words together to express a complete thought by the age of three.

Medical professionals make a distinction between expressive language disorder (where speech is affected but comprehension is normal) and mixed receptive-expressive language disorder (where both speech and comprehension are affected).

Characteristics of expressive language disorder include extremely poor vocabulary, confusion regarding vocabulary and verb inflections that express the concepts of past and future, the phenomenon of knowing what one wants to say but being unable to recall the required words, and difficulty speaking at length. Mixed receptive-expressive language disorder is characterized by all of the above, plus other symptoms such as an inability to take dictation and difficulty comprehending specific classes of vocabulary, such as prepositions indicating location (e.g., in, above, etc.).

Frequently asked questions

Is the incidence of high-functioning developmental disorders increasing?

"There must have been children with high-functioning developmental disorders in generations past, but I had never even heard of such a thing until recently. What is going on?" One possible answer to this question is that such cases have always existed in similar numbers, but that in the past fewer teachers, parents, and physicians were focusing on these children's problems in a proactive way. A second possibility is that advances in assessment standards have contributed to an increase in the number of cases diagnosed.

Are these "milder" conditions really such a problem?

The short answer to this question is yes—the reason being that, by definition, even a mild developmental disorder would never be officially diagnosed as such unless the child were actually having conspicuous difficulty with everyday activities or social relationships.

For example, take the case of a child who has difficulty concentrating and occasionally gets up and wanders around a bit during class. Such a child would not be diagnosed as having ADHD if he or she were able to concentrate and complete assignments when allowed several rest breaks and were able to return to his or her seat and attend to the lesson when asked to do so. A diagnosis, then, is part of a coordinated effort to give a child help that is genuinely needed; if the child is managing reasonably well, then a diagnostic label and medical intervention are simply not necessary.

It is also good to remember that a child with a developmental disorder should be seen as *having* a problem, not as *being* a problem. We diagnose and treat because the effects of the disorder put the individual at a number of disadvantages, not because these effects result in inconvenience to others. The proper attitude consists of wanting to benefit the child, not "fix" the child.

A few final words

Unfortunately, children with developmental disorders are likely to suffer from high levels of stress due to having to cope with the usual demands of everyday life. It is therefore very important that parents and other adults who play a supportive role in the child's life accurately understand the child's developmental characteristics and provide appropriate help. Unbalanced development, in and of itself, is not a problem; cast in a more positive light, it can simply be considered an expression of distinctive individuality. Adults, therefore, should choose forms of assistance that will serve the specific purpose of making life more pleasant and satisfying for the child. For example, in environments where exuberance and energetic activity are welcomed, children with ADHD fit right in and have no need whatsoever of special intervention. Concepts like "disorder" and "handicap," sadly, are in one sense merely social constructs. What is considered a disorder in a given culture might come to be seen as entirely normal if that culture were to change. This type of change is the *sine qua non* of a truly barrier-free society; it requires that the burden of accommodation be borne by the majority of individuals who are not adversely affected by "disorders" or "unusual characteristics" with the goal being to enable affected individuals to live on an equal footing.

It is not appropriate to expect children with developmental disorders to simply overcome their difficulties by sheer strength of will, without any efforts by others to accommodate them. Would this be asked of a blind person? Of course not. In both cases, it is up to us to do our part.

Our agenda should not be specifically to produce children who can sit still in class, write legibly, or anything of the sort. Instead, it should be to enable these children to experience more days filled with joy rather than pain.

All children have the right to experience happiness *now*, without having to wait for some unspecified time in the future. If more, not fewer, of their yesterdays, todays, and tomorrows are spent pleasantly, then children with developmental disorders will eventually arrive at adulthood in a state of psychological well-being. And this should be the ultimate goal of any intervention offered in support of a child's development.